Report

The Nones:
Who are they and what do they believe?

Hannah Waite

Acknowledgements

First, I would like to thank my Theos colleagues for their insight and feedback on this report. In particular, Emily Downe for the beautiful illustrations and Nick Spencer, thank you for all your wisdom and careful consideration in the research, writing and editing of this report.

I would like to offer my sincere thanks to Professor Stephen Bullivant for his thoughtful comments on an earlier draft and for your kind and encouraging words in the Foreword of this report. A final thanks to Vern Farewell for his guidance on the statistical components of this research.

This report is the result of data collected from a three-year project conducted by Theos and The Faraday Institute for Science and Religion, and funded by the Templeton Religion Trust on the landscape of science and religion in the UK. I would like to thank the Templeton Religion Trust for their generous funding of the project.

Foreword

Perhaps the most striking fact about religion in Britain is that over half of the adult population say that they don't belong to one. When the annual British Social Attitudes survey began in 1983, the proportion with 'no religion' was already as high as 31%. It had hit 40% by the mid-1990s, then first tipped 50% in 2009. It's remained stubbornly there or thereabouts ever since: 53% in 2019, for example.

Given just how large the 'Nones' segment of the population is, it is – or ought to be – surprising just how little we actually know about them. Indeed, it is only in the past ten or fifteen years that they've received much study from social scientists at all. There are have been some excellent, in-depth studies in this time – Lois Lee's 2015 book Recognizing the Non-religious: Reimagining the Secular (Oxford University Press) being a particular stand-out. But what we haven't had, and what we've really needed, is a fullscale, tailor-made nationally representative survey.

Until now, that is.

Thanks to Theos, we finally have a None-specific quantitative study: wide-ranging, carefully designed by experts (and in consultation with many others), with over 5000 respondents, and fielded by one of the country's top polling companies. And what's more, we also have this fascinating, clearly written analysis by Hannah Waite.

It is not the place of a Foreword writer to give spoilers. More's the pity, as there are plenty of intriguing, illuminating findings here that I'm eager to start writing about.

In short, this is a valuable new source of both data and insight in making sense of the (non)religious lives of over half (and a significantly higher percentage than that of the younger segments) of British adults.

Stephen Bullivant
Professor of Theology and the Sociology of Religion, St Mary's University, UK
Professorial Research Fellow in Theology and Sociology, University of Notre Dame, Australia

September 2022

This report in 30 seconds

Around half of Britons now categorise themselves as having "No Religion"; these are colloquially known as 'Nones'. But having no religion does not mean having no beliefs. It doesn't even mean having no religious beliefs.

This report explores the demography, beliefs and practices of Nones and then presents a cluster analysis of this group. It shows that Nones comprise a complex and sometimes counter-intuitive group with, for example, only 51% of them stating they "don't believe in God," and 42% believing in some form of the supernatural.

This report demonstrates that there are three distinctive types or clusters of Nones. Each cluster displays varying degrees of belief about religion, knowledge, God and spirituality. In essence, "Campaigning Nones" are self-consciously atheistic and hostile to religion; "Tolerant Nones" are broadly atheistic but accepting of (sometimes warm towards) religion; and "Spiritual Nones", who are characterised by a range of spiritual beliefs and practices, as much as many people who tick the "Religion" box.

Contents

Contents

Figures and Tables

Executive Summary

— Around half of adults in the UK now say that they have "No Religion" (i.e. are Nones).

— Individuals under 50 years old are more likely to identify as non-religious.

— Millennials (Millennials are defined as those born in 1981 – 1996, at the time of data collection this was individuals aged from 24 - 39) are disproportionately more likely to be Nones than other generation.

— There are slightly more males who identify as None than females (54% vs 46% of women).

— Only 51% of those who identify as non-religious state, "I don't believe in God." 14% believe in a higher power and 9% believe in God more or less firmly.

— 36% of Nones believe that "Humans are at heart spiritual beings" (vs 49% of overall population).

— 42% of Nones believe in some form of the supernatural.

— Nones believe more readily in aspects of New Age Spirituality rather than classically religious beliefs.

  — 17% of Nones believe in the power of prayer, 16% in reincarnation, 14% in the healing power of crystals, and 14% in the supernatural power of ancestors.
  — A fifth (20%) of Nones state they definitely/ probably believe in life after death (vs 37% of total population), and 27% of Nones believe in ghosts (vs 36% of total population) but only 11% believe in Heaven.

— The overall group of Nones naturally divides into three sub-groups which we have called Spiritual Nones, Campaigning Nones and Tolerant Nones.

— Spiritual Nones represent 32% of the population of the Nones. They are much more likely to be women than men. They are:

  — spiritually open
  — less atheistic and more agnostic in their belief about God
  — more likely to believe in a higher power of some form than a personal God
  — accepting of religion
  — individuals who see value in religion and its place in the modern world
  — individuals who believe that science is only able to describe and explain part of reality

— Campaigning Nones represent 34% of the population of the Nones. They are much more likely to be men than women. They are:

  — spiritually closed (only 20% hold any form of spiritual belief)
  — individuals who believe science is the only reliable way to describe, explain and understand reality
  — strongly atheistic (80% are atheists)
  — extremely hostile to religion (78% believe it is comparable to smallpox, vs 29% of Nones overall)
  — a group of individuals who see no value in religion or its place in society

— Tolerant Nones represent 35% of the population of the Nones. They are slightly younger than the other groups but have no particular gender imbalance. They:

  — have the highest levels of education out of all the clusters

— are spiritually closed
— are generally atheistic in their belief about God, although around a quarter are agnostic
— believe that science cannot tell you how to live your life
— are more tolerant and accepting of religion than Campaigning Nones
— believe religion has some helpful things to say about ethics.

Introduction

For the first time in – well – ever, half of the British population say that they have no religion. Public opinion polling, such as the survey on which this report is based, commonly reports that more than half of the population has no religion.[1]

Not only is this historically unprecedented but it is also geographically highly unusual. Some countries – Czech Republic, China, North Korea and Japan for example – have long boasted more than half of their population as non-religious (or 'unaffiliated').[2] Nevertheless, this level of Nones is still high by European standards[3] let alone by the standards of a world that is not only predominantly religious but also growing more so.[4]

The raw data themselves, however, pose more questions than they answer, and perhaps the most significant of these is: what does this actually mean?

When, in 1983, the first British Social Attitude survey asked people about their religious affiliation and reported that 40% of the population said they belonged to the Church of England, a number of commentators wondered where they all were on a Sunday morning. There appeared to be some 17-18 million people missing from the pews. In a similar vein, when the 2001 Census reported 71% of the population of England and Wales as Christian, others asked how many of them read the Bible, confessed faith in Jesus Christ or even believed in God. In other words, although the religious category you place yourself in does mean something, it doesn't mean everything. Self-designation is *a* measure of religiosity but not the only measure and certainly not the most reliable.

As with religion, so with non-religion. If, as seems likely now, we are moving to a majority of the UK being non-religious, it is important to ask what exactly that means. This is what this report does. By drawing on an extensive quantitative survey conducted by YouGov around the time of the 2021 Census, it allows us to look "under the bonnet" of non-religion in UK today. What it finds is telling.

As with the "Church of England" box in 1983, or the "Christian" box in 2001, the "Non-Religious" box of 2021 is a mixed one. It includes the passionate, committed, indeed campaigning non-believers, who know their Dawkins chapter and verse, sing songs in atheist churches, and tithe faithfully to the National Secular Society. But it also includes those whose beliefs (and even sometimes practices) are all but indistinguishable from many who tick the religion box, as well as those for whom none of this really matters very much, or others who are like Winston Churchill, supporting the Church as a buttress rather than pillar (i.e. from the outside rather than from within). The belief of the Nones is like that of the Faithful, a complex thing.

There will no doubt be much more reflection on this topic over the coming years, as academic focus on this phenomenon continues to grow. We hope that these data and this report provide a useful contribution to understanding the rapidly changing non-religious landscape of Britain.

Hannah Waite

A note on data

This report draws on the results of a quantitative survey of 5,153 UK adults conducted by YouGov on behalf of Theos and The Faraday Institute for Science and Religion between 5th May and 13th June 2021, a month or so after the 2021 UK Census.

The research was conducted using an online interview, developed by Theos, The Faraday Institute and YouGov, and administered to members of the YouGov Plc UK panel of 800,000+ individuals who have agreed to take part in surveys. Responses were weighted accordingly to make up a demographically representative national sample.

1   At the time of writing, the relevant results of the 2021 Census had yet to be published.

2   Pew Research Center, Pew Research Center, 'The Global Religious Landscape', *A Pew Forum on Religion and Public Life Report*, (December 2012) assets. pewresearch.org/wp-content/uploads/sites/11/2014/01/global-religion-full. pdf

3   Jonathan Evans and Chris Baronavski, 'How do European Countries differ in religious commitment?', *Pew Research Center*, (5 Dec 2018) www.pewresearch.org/fact-tank/2018/12/05/ how-do-european-countries-differ-in-religious-commitment/

4   Pew Research Center, 'The Future of World Religions', (2 April 2015) www. pewresearch.org/religion/2015/04/02/religious-projections-2010-2050/

1. The Rise of the Nones

"The state of lacking (especially religious) faith or belief... unbelief is often used in a wide sense, implying generalized lack of belief in a God of gods."[1]

Over the last 50 years, the number who identify as non-religious in the UK population has grown drastically. In fact, the non-religious are the fastest growing group in the country according to the Office of National Statistics (ONS).[2]

In the 2011 Census, 25% of adults in England and Wales identified as non-religious, a number that is sure to rise with the publication of the 2021 Census. Over the intervening period, the British Social Attitudes (BSA) survey has continued to track the rapid growth of the non-religious population, recording higher levels of non-religiosity than the Census. Thus, according to BSA, from 31% of the population in 1983 to 43% in 2015, by 2018 over half (53%) of the British public described themselves as non-religious.[3]

Although not published at the time of writing, the 2021 Census is widely expected to track the trend towards 50% seen in the BSA data.

'Atheist' vs 'None'

With the number of people in Britain who now identify as non-religious steadily rising, we need to consider what is actually meant by the term non-religious?

It is important to tease out the nuances of the Nones, as people often assume that those who tick None are straightforwardly atheists. The fact is, however, that atheism and being non-religious do not always go hand in hand, and one can be non-religious without being an atheist.

This implicit understanding that being non-religious means you are an atheist can do a disservice to those who place themselves within the None box but are not straightforwardly atheists. Misunderstanding the Nones in this way means we lose a great deal of nuance and insight into those who do not fit this picture. The purpose of this report is to disambiguate the None category and show that those who are non-religious are not necessarily all of one "flavour". Rather, there are a variety of flavours and ways to be non-religious that do not fit within the defined "Atheist" box.[4]

The data and argument of this report are in line with, and build upon, the work of Dr Lois Lee, whose research highlights that the None category can at times, wrongly be used as a "catch-all."[5] It is not simply a category for those who are atheists, but also those who are agnostic or, as we shall see, spiritual in their beliefs.

Simply, the non-religious (the Nones) are those who tick the non-religious box (or its various other forms). None is a mark of affiliation, one that contrasts with the affiliation to

religion(s). In this sense, the term None does not necessarily indicate what an individual does or does not believe. Rather, it is a social marker, a way to identify oneself. It is a mark of affiliation, and just like many groups, there are different flavours of those who identify as non-religious.

There are a variety of flavours and ways to be non-religious.

It is the hope of this research to provide further clarification on what these different "flavours" are and, in particular, what Nones believe about God, spirituality, the supernatural, religion and its role within society.

Who are the Nones?

We asked UK adult respondents, "Do you regard yourself as belonging to any particular religion, and if so, to which of these do you belong?" Participants were able to select:

— No – I do not regard myself as belonging to any particular religion.

— Yes – with the options of Christianity (including several denominations), Hinduism, Islam, Buddhism, Judaism, Sikhism, and "Prefer not to say" (see questionnaire on Theos website for full details).[6]

The data compiled for this report is analysed from those who selected "No, I do not regard myself as belonging to any particular religion" (n = 2705).

We found that more men identify as a None than women; 54% of men vs 46% of women define themselves as a None. Male representation in the Nones is higher than the overall population, which consists of 49% of men and 51% of women.[7]

Individuals under 50 years old are more likely to identify as non-religious. This is in line with previous research from the 2011 Census which found that the majority of those who identify as non-religious were under 50.[8]

Likewise, previous data demonstrated that 16–29-year-olds are the least religious, not just in UK but also across Europe.[9] The current research follows this trend with 27% of the non-religious being 16–29-year-olds. We found that these age differences coincide with a significant generational difference (Figure 1). This shows that Millennials (those born in 1981 – 1996, at the time of data collection, this was individuals aged from 24-39) make up the majority of the Nones. It also shows, however, that while Millennials are proportionately more likely to call themselves Nones (i.e. Millennials comprise 32% of the population but 37% of Nones), there is less of a difference among Gen Z (those born from 1997 onward, at the time of data collection aged 18-23) who comprise c. 9-10% of the population and 9-10% of Nones.

Figure 1: Generations of the Nones

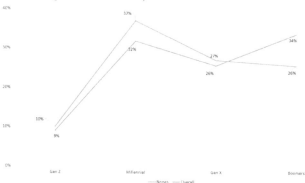

Source: Theos/ Faraday/ YouGov 2022: [(Nones [n = 2705], Overall Population [n= 5153])

What do they believe about...religion?

Nones do not call themselves religious – by definition. But what do they think about religion?

We asked respondents several questions regarding religion. Questions covered topics such as the truthfulness of religion, its place within society, and whether it was viewed in either a negative or a positive way.

When asked on a standard five-point scale of strongly agree to strongly disagree, 36% of Nones strongly agree or agree (heretofore referred to as strongly/ agree) that "All religions have some element

❝

36% of Nones strongly agree or agree that "All religions have some element of truth in them".

of truth in them", compared to 50% of the overall population. The results also showed that 35% of Nones disagree with this statement (vs 24% of the overall sample). Nones, therefore, are naturally more sceptical of religion, but being a None does not necessarily mean rejecting or disparaging all elements of religious belief or truth.[10]

On the surface, it might seem obvious that the Nones would believe that religion – something that they deliberately do not affiliate with – should have no place in the modern world.

However, the data show that a third of Nones (33%) disagree that "Religion has no place in the modern world" (Figure 2).

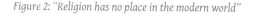

Figure 2: "Religion has no place in the modern world"

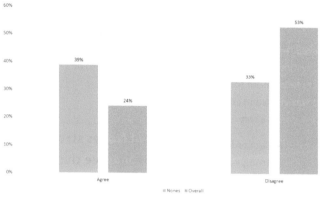

Source: Theos/ Faraday/ YouGov 2022: Q2c_3, (Nones [n =2705], Overall Population [n= 5153])

We also explored the strength of Nones hostility to religion, by putting to them several famous statements made by Britain's leading anti-religious thinker, Richard Dawkins, to the effect that religion is comparable to the smallpox virus but harder to eradicate[11] and also that "Religion is a form of child abuse".[12]

We found that 29% of Nones agree that "Religion is comparable to the smallpox virus but harder to eradicate" and 24% believe that "Religion is a form of child abuse" (Figure 3). These are, predictably, higher levels of antagonism towards religion than among the overall population. However, the data show that real anti-religious hostility is still limited among Nones. In fact, Nones who hold extremely antagonistic views of religion are the minority.

Figure 3: Nones' views on religion

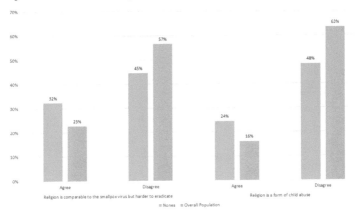

Source: Theos/ Faraday/ YouGov 2022: Q2c_6 and Q2c_7, (Nones [n = 2705], Overall Population [n =5153])

Exploring why Nones are not religious is difficult for quantitative work, as it requires a careful qualitative probing of articulated and assumed beliefs. However, we were able to explore the extent to which science was considered the barrier to religion. We found that science does appear to impact an individual's opinion of religion, with 45% of Nones agreeing that "Science has disproved religion" vs 32% of the overall population (Figure 4).

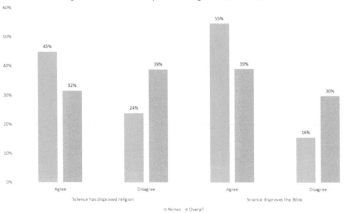

Figure 4: "Science disproves religion and the Bible"

Source: Theos/ Faraday/ YouGov 2022: Q5_4 and Q5_8 (Nones [n = 2705], Overall Population [n= 5153])

Nones, by and large, not only hold a negative view of religion, but believe that science has both disproved religion and the Bible.[13]

It is no surprise to learn that the majority of Nones (39%) view the Bible as "An irrelevant collection of ancient myths" and, as you would expect, this figure is higher than the overall population (Figure 5). However, it may be surprising to learn that nearly a quarter of Nones (23%) describe the Bible as "A useful book of guidance and advice for our lives but not the Word of God". A further 15% stated that they view the Bible as "Beautiful literature but otherwise irrelevant to us today," and 18% stated they did not have a view on this.[14]

Figure 5: Nones' feelings about the Bible

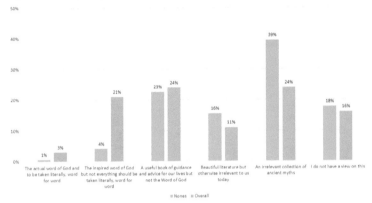

Source: Theos/ Faraday/ YouGov 2022: Q17 (Nones [n =2705], Overall Population [n= 5153])

What do they believe about... God and the supernatural?

In culture, society and the "popular mind", the term non-religious and atheist are often conflated. In this way, many people believe that Nones simply do not believe in God. However, we found that only 51% of those who identify as non-religious state "I don't believe in God" (Figure 6). In a similar vein, we found that there is a significant percentage of Nones who believe in some form of God/ higher power.[15]

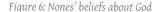

Figure 6: Nones' beliefs about God

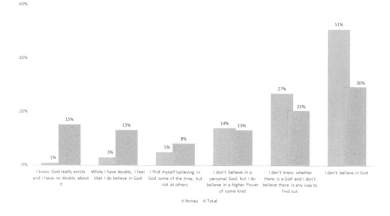

Source: Theos/ Faraday/ YouGov 2022: Q16 (Nones [n =2705], Overall Population [n= 5153])

Just like any religious group, the non-religious population vary in their degrees of non-belief. 14% of Nones believe in a form of higher power and a further 27% are straightforwardly agnostic, not knowing (or believing there is a way to know) either way. A minority of Nones (c. 9%) believe in God, more or less firmly.

As we continue to unpack what it really means to be a None, it becomes clearer that Nones are not simply focused on science and materialism. Rather, we found that 36% of Nones agree, "Humans are at heart spiritual beings" (vs 49% of overall population), and 42% of those who identify as "None" believe in some form of the supernatural[16] (Figure 7).

Figure 7: Nones' levels of belief in the supernatural / spiritual

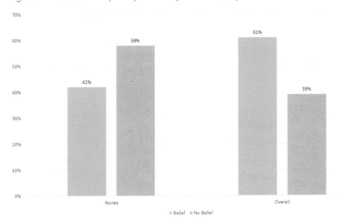

Source: Theos/ Faraday/ YouGov 2022: Q23_all (Nones [n = 2705], Overall Population [n= 5153])

Given that at least two in five Nones believe in something spiritual, it appears that Nones are indeed a more spiritual group than perhaps previously thought. It certainly appears that many of the individuals within this group straddle the line of non-belief and being "Spiritual but not religious" (SBNR).

Perhaps this finding is indicative of the age of Nones, as it has been well documented that those aged 23-39, (aka Millennials) are leaving religion behind.[17] Alternatively, could this rise in spiritual belief of the Nones be due to the rise of new age spirituality/ spiritual wellness in popular culture and on social media?[18]

Two in five Nones believe in something spiritual.

We found that Nones believe more readily in aspects of New Age Spirituality rather than classically religious spiritual or supernatural beliefs. A fifth (20%) of Nones state they definitely/ probably believe in life after death (vs 37% of total population), but only 11% of Nones believe in Heaven and 9% in Hell. We see then that while 1 in 5 Nones believe in life after death, it is not in a traditionally Judeo-Christian religious sense.

Instead, we found that 27% of Nones believe in ghosts (vs. 36% of total population). Is this, then, the way in which Nones understand life after death? Not through belief in a form of heaven or hell, but rather through belief in ghosts, which are by their very nature, understood to be the soul or the spirit of an individual that remains on earth after they have died. If we pair this finding with the fact that 36% of Nones believe that humans are at heart spiritual beings, it seems that some Nones believe in the soul/ spiritual component of an individual, and that once an individual dies they experience life after death as their soul remains on earth and they are "ghosts".

We found that following belief in ghosts, 17% of Nones believe in the "power of prayer", and a further 16% believe in reincarnation. Finally, we found that 14% of Nones believe in angels, the healing power of crystals and the supernatural power of ancestors respectively. It is interesting that although Nones are more likely to believe in ghosts than any other form of supernatural occurrences, a minority of Nones do still believe in certain classically religious beliefs, such as the power of prayer and angels.

Overall, it certainly appears that the majority of Nones who do believe in the supernatural/ spiritual subscribe more to 'New Age' spirituality, or a different (i.e. non-Abrahamic) understanding of religion, with more Nones believing in ghosts, the healing power of crystals, reincarnation, and the supernatural power of ancestors. Perhaps even angels fall into this category with aspects of new age spirituality discussing angels in a new sense.

What we do know is that Nones who are spiritual and believe in the supernatural believe less in classically religious connotations of spirituality such as heaven and hell, but are comfortable with the idea of prayer and angels, and are also more comfortable with non-religious understandings of spirituality and the supernatural.

Conclusion

Throughout our investigation into the Nones it is clear that this group of individuals are not nearly as "clear cut" as we sometimes believe. Rather, we have found a richness and diversity in who the Nones are and what they believe. For example, we found that 51% of Nones are atheist, while a further 27% are agnostic and 23% are believers in some form of God/ gods or a higher power. This is a far cry from the idea that non-religion equates to outright disbelief and disregard of anything supernatural or spiritual (although it is important to stress that half of the Nones do fall within this category).

1   Stephen Bullivant and Lois Lee, *The Oxford Dictionary of Atheism*, (Oxford University Press, 2016), 10.1093/acref/9780191816819.001.0001

2   Office for National Statistics, 'Religion by Local Authority, Great Britain, 2011 to 2018', (London: ONS, 5 April 2019) www.ons.gov.uk/peoplepopulationandcommunity/culturalidentity/religion/adhocs/009830religionbylocalauthoritygreatbritain2011to2018

3   David Voas and Steve Bruce, 'Religion: Identity, behaviour and belief over two decades' in J. Curtice, E. Clery, J, Perry, M. Phillips and N. Rahim, (eds.) *British Social Attitudes: the 36th Report* (London: the National Centre for Social Research, 2019)

4   For further insight into these different modes of being Non-Religious and the rise of the Nones please see:
Lois Lee, *Recognizing the Non-religious: Reimagining the Secular*, (Oxford University Press, 2015); Lois Lee, "Ambivalent Atheist Identities: Power and Non-religious Culture in Contemporary Britain", in Ruy Llera Blanes and Galina Oustinova-Stjepanovic (eds.) *Being Godless: Ethnographies of Atheism and Non-Religion*, (New York and Oxford: Barghan Books); Stephen Bullivant, Miguel Farias, Jonathan Lanman and Lois Less, *Understanding Unbelief: Atheists and agnostics around the world*, (St Mary's University Twickenham, 2019); Stephen Bullivant, "The "No Religion" Population of Britain: Recent Data from the British Social Attitudes Survey (2015) and the European Social Survey (2014)" (*Benedict XVI Centre for Religion and Society*, 2017); Linda Woodhead, "The rise of 'No Religion' in Britain: The emergence of a new cultural majority", *The British Academy Lecture, 19th January 2016*; Linda Woodhead, "The rise of 'No Religion': Towards an Explanation", Sociology of Religion, 78 Vol 3, (2017) p. 247-262.

5   Lois Lee, "Secular or Nonreligious? Investigating and Interpreting Generic 'Not Religious' Categories and Populations", Taylor and Frances online, (2014), pp. 466-482, Episode 8: Science and Non-Religion with Dr Lois Lee, on the Science and Belief in Society Podcast www.scienceandbeliefinsociety.org/2021/05/04/episode-8-science-and-non-religion-with-dr-lois-lee/, What do Unbelievers Actually Believe? Dr. Lois Lee, John Templeton Foundation, www.youtube.com/watch?v=lp8DkzXOG7M

6   We have taken this question from the British Social Attitudes Survey. 5, in comparison to the Census question regarding religion. The Census question has come under criticism (especially from Humanists UK) as the wording assumes that the default position of the public is that they are religious asking "What is your religion?" However, the BSA question does not present similar levels of assumption and is a more neutral way to ask the same question.

7   We found no other significant demographic differences from the overall population.

8 www.ons.gov.uk/peoplepopulationandcommunity/culturalidentity/religion/
   articles/exploringreligioninenglandandwales/february2020

9 Stephen Bullivant, 'Europe's Young Adults and Religion: Findings from the
   European Social Survey (2014-16) to inform the 2018 Synod of Bishops' (2018).

10 However, it is worth noting that the statement is generic and does not give
   inference to the aspect of religions that individuals may believe are truthful.

11 In a speech given to the American Humanist Association in 1996, Dawkins
   stated. "A case can be made that faith is one of the world's great evils,
   comparable to the smallpox virus, but harder to eradicate." See Richard
   Dawkins, "Is Science a Religion?" The Humanist, 57 Vol 1 (1997), p.26-29.

12 Rob Cooper, "'Forcing a Religion on Your Children Is as Bad as Child Abuse,
   Claims Atheist Professor Richard Dawkins,'" The Daily Mail (23 April, 2013)
   www.dailymail.co.uk/news/article-2312813/Richard-Dawkins-Forcing-
   religion-children-child-abuse-claims-atheist-professor.html

13 We also asked respondents to what extent do they agree / disagree that
   "Science disproves the Qur'an". With 16% of Nones agreeing that science
   disproves the Qur'an (11% disagreeing, and 22% neither agreeing nor
   disagreeing with this statement), and 39% selecting "don't know". When
   removing the "don't know" we found that of those who voiced an opinion, 26%
   of Nones agree that science disprove the Qur'an vs 18% who disagree with this
   statement. This result while interesting, is not statistically significant when
   the "don't know" are removed.

14 Individuals were also asked about their views of the Qur'an, with the majority
   of individuals (44%) stating they do not have a view on the Qur'an, and a
   further 31% view the Qur'an as an irrelevant collection of ancient myths. A
   further 12% view the Qur'an as a useful book of guidance and advice for our
   lives but not the Word of God, and 10% as beautiful literature that is otherwise
   irrelevant to us today.

15 Exactly what people mean by "a higher power" is unclear. It could be
   interpreted as fate, or destiny, or providence, or the universe. The Dutch have
   a term, *ietsisme*, literally understood as "somethingism", which captures this.
   Either way, the term is a commonly used but intentionally vague placeholder.
   We are grateful for Stephen Bullivant for his comments on this.

16 We asked individuals on four-point scale (definitely, probably, probably not
   and definitely not) to what extent do they believe in: life after death, heaven,
   hell, religious miracles, reincarnation, nirvana, angels, ghosts, the power of
   prayer, the healing power of crystals and the supernatural power of ancestors.
   In exploring these different dimensions of the spiritual and supernatural, we
   found that 42% of Nones believed in at least one from the list above.

17 www.pewresearch.org/religion/2018/06/13/
   young-adults-around-the-world-are-less-religious-by-several-measures/

18 Nana Baah, 'Manifesting is Gen Z's Answer to New Age Spirituality' Vice, 16 March 2022 www.vice.com/en/article/qjbn43/manifesting-is-gen-zs-answer-to-new-age-spirituality, Stuart McGurk, 'Making dreams come true: inside the age world of manifesting' The Guardian, 20 March 2022; www.theguardian.com/lifeandstyle/2022/mar/20/making-dreams-come-true-inside-the-new-age-world-of-manifesting

2. Different Types of None

The data in chapter 1 made it clear that the Nones – religiously and spiritually speaking – are a more varied and interesting group than the superficial picture of them suggests. To understand this variety and complexity, we analysed the data further to assess if there were different groupings or clusters there.

Methodology

To begin with, we took the 2,705 respondents who fit within the parameters of a None. Twenty-one variables were selected for this process of segmentation. Once these variables had been selected, we began data cleaning by removing respondents who did not answer one or more of the 21 variables. The complete data set was 1,883 and it was these remaining respondents that were used for segmentation analysis.

We decided that a cluster analysis would provide the most robust insight into the Nones data. A cluster analysis is a statistical method used to group similar responses into representative clusters. Simply, it is a way to divide the responses of the Nones into several groups according to similar responses to selected questions. The aim of this analysis was to organise the data into meaningful groups to identify if there were different typologies of Nones.[1]

To begin our cluster analysis, we selected 21 statements upon which to base the clusters.[2]

We identified three distinct clusters:[3]

1   Cluster one (n = 601): represents 32% of the population of the Nones. People in this cluster strongly believe in spirituality and some form of supernatural.

2   Cluster two (n = 618): represents 34% of the population of
     the Nones. People in this cluster are strongly antagonistic
     towards religion, and do not believe in spirituality/
     supernatural.

3   Cluster three (n = 664): represents 35% of the population
     of the Nones. People in this cluster hold a more tolerant
     or accepting view of religion than those in cluster two
     but they have none of the spiritual interest of those in
     cluster 1.

We found no significant differences between clusters
regarding the following demographic information: age/
generation, terminal level of science education, or terminal
level of religious education. However, we did find a significant
difference in cluster populations when it came to gender and
terminal age of formal education.

'SPIRITUAL NONES'

Cluster 1. Spiritual Nones

The first cluster we identified is what we have called the *Spiritual Nones*.

The Spiritual Nones:

— Are spiritually open;
— Believe that science is only able to describe and explain part of reality;
— Are less atheistic and more agnostic in their belief about God;
— Are more likely to believe in a higher power of some form than in a personal God;
— Are accepting of religion;
— See some value in religion and its place in the modern world.

Table 1: Generational Trends of Overall Population, Nones Overall and Spiritual Nones

	Overall Population	Nones Overall	Spiritual Nones
Gen Z	9%	10%	11%
Millennial	32%	37%	35%
Gen X	26%	27%	31%
Boomers	34%	26%	23%

Source: Theos/ Faraday/ YouGov 2022: Overall Population [n = 5153], Nones [n = 2705], Spiritual Nones [n = 601]

When it comes to age, we found that Spiritual Nones follow a similar generational trend as Nones overall, with the majority of them being Millennials, followed by Gen X. However, we noticed that Spiritual Nones also have proportionately more Gen X individuals, and proportionately fewer Boomers than Nones overall and than the overall population.

Spiritual Nones are disproportionately women (61% women vs 39% men), with the age balance following that of the overall population of Nones. People in this group have a lower level of science knowledge than Nones overall, with only 31% of Spiritual Nones obtaining a high science knowledge score compared to 44% of Nones overall.

80% of Spiritual Nones believe in some form of the supernatural/spiritual.

Their spirituality

The Spiritual Nones are different from other Nones due to their beliefs in the spiritual and supernatural. A full 80% of Spiritual Nones believe in some form of the supernatural/ spiritual.[4] When asked if they agree or disagree with the statement, "Humans are at heart spiritual beings," we found that a majority (61%) of them agree with this statement compared with 36% of the overall population of Nones.

Spiritual Nones are not only the most open to the possibility of the supernatural but are also most open to other forms of epistemology, or ways of knowing the world.

Their attitude to knowledge

We found that 64% of Spiritual Nones agree that "Science is only able to explain part of reality", and 77% agree, "There are some things science will never be able to explain" (Figure 8).

Figure 8: Beliefs about the boundaries of what science can explain: by Nones Cluster

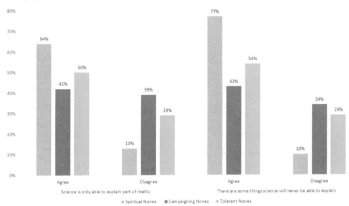

Source: Theos/ Faraday/ YouGov 2022: Q1_5, 1_8 (Spiritual Nones [n= 601], Campaigning Nones [n = 618], Tolerant Nones [n = 664])

The data appears to suggest that Spiritual Nones believe that there are other relevant, insightful, and truthful forms of knowledge than just that provided by science. In this sense, Spiritual Nones do not recognise science as the only form of authoritative knowledge that can teach us valuable insights about the world, or that science is the ultimate discipline that will one day be able to explain everything. Instead, Spiritual Nones are what we would call epistemological pluralists, meaning they believe that there are many different (relevant and fulfilling) ways to understand the world and science is just one of them.

Spiritual Nones are epistemological pluralists.

It seems that epistemological pluralism may play a significant role in why this group of individuals are more open to the notion of the spiritual and the supernatural. In Theos' report _Science and Religion: Moving away from the shallow end,_ we established that an individual's epistemology can pre-determine their views of science and religion, and in this case, their opinions towards religion. If an individual believes strongly that science is the _only_ way to gain factual and truthful evidence about the world, they are very unlikely to believe in a spiritual or supernatural realm. However, if an individual believes there are other forms of knowledge and there is more than a physical reality or materialism, it makes sense that they would be more open to the notion of the spiritual/ supernatural, God or a higher power, and in effect, be more agreeable to religion. This does not mean that individuals within this group are religious. Rather, it demonstrates that because of their epistemological framework they may value and accept religion and its place in society more than those who hold a staunch scientific epistemological framework.

Their belief about God

We found that Spiritual Nones have more varied beliefs about God compared to overall Nones (Figure 9).

Figure 9: Spiritual Nones' beliefs about God

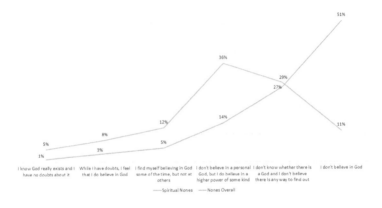

Source: Theos/ Faraday/ YouGov 2022: Q16 [(Nones [n = 2705], Spiritual Nones [n =601])

In this way, the Spiritual Nones provide a vastly different picture of belief in God from the overall view of the Nones, with only 11% of Spiritual Nones stating they do not believe in God (vs 51% of Nones overall).

Similarly, 12% of Spiritual Nones select, "I find myself believing in God some of the time, but not at others". 29% claim to be agnostic, stating "I don't know whether there is a God and I don't believe there is any way to find out," and a further 36% believe not in a personal God but a higher power of some kind. Furthermore, 13% of Spiritual Nones believe in God (selecting either "I know God really exists and I have no doubts about it" or "While I have doubts, I feel that I do believe in God") and a further 12% say that "I find myself believing in God some of the time, but not at others".

Their belief about the Bible and religion

Spiritual Nones hold varied views about the Bible, with 34% viewing it as "a useful book of guidance and advice for our lives but not the word of God", compared with 23% of Nones overall who hold this position. By comparison, only a fifth of Spiritual Nones think that the Bible is "an irrelevant collection of ancient myths", vs 39% of Nones overall who take this view. In a similar vein, Spiritual Nones are three times more likely than the Nones overall to say that they think the Bible is the inspired but not literal word of God (11% vs 4%) (Figure 10).

Figure 10: Spiritual Nones' beliefs about the Bible

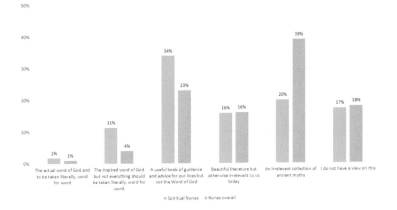

Source: Theos/ Faraday/ YouGov 2022: Q17 (Nones [n =2705], Spiritual Nones [n= 601])

This finding underlines the lower levels of hostility that Spiritual Nones have towards religion, with 57% disagreeing that "Religion has no place in the modern world" (Figure 11). Spiritual Nones are not only open to forms of spirituality, the supernatural, and God, but also to the role of religion within the public square.

Figure 11: "Religion has no place in the modern world": by Nones Cluster

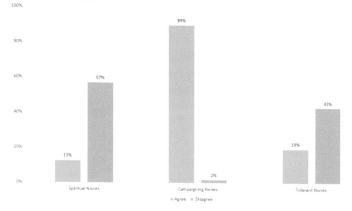

Source: Theos/ Faraday/ YouGov 2022: Q2c_3 (Spiritual Nones [n= 601], Campaigning Nones [n= 618], Tolerant Nones [n = 664])

Spiritual Nones not only hold a more positive view of religion in society, but a further 59% agree that "All religions have some element of truth in them" compared to only 36% of Nones overall.

This trend is bolstered by the fact that that 55% of Spiritual Nones disagree with the statement "Religion has nothing helpful to say about ethics" compared with 16% of Nones overall who disagree. Spiritual Nones appear to hold the view that not only does religion possess certain types of truth, and valuable insights into ethical matters but that it is because of these views that religion has a valued place in society.

Spiritual Nones demonstrate that a considerable proportion of Nones take spirituality seriously and are accepting of religion and its place in the modern world.

Summary

Spiritual Nones play an important part in our understanding of the diversity of opinions in the Nones more fully. This cluster demonstrates that Nones are not simply individuals who are anti-religion or even anti-spirituality. Rather, the Spiritual Nones demonstrate that a considerable proportion of Nones take spirituality seriously and are accepting of religion and its place in the modern world.

'CAMPAIGNING NONES'

Cluster 2. Campaigning Nones

The second cluster that we identified was those whom we have named **Campaigning Nones.**

Campaigning Nones:

— Are spiritually closed;
— Believe science is the only reliable way to describe, explain and understand reality;
— Are extremely atheistic;
— Are extremely hostile to religion;
— See no value in religion or its place in society.

Table 2: Generational Trends of Overall Population, Nones Overall and Campaigning Nones

	Overall Population	Nones Overall	Campaigning Nones
Gen Z	9%	10%	7%
Millennial	32%	37%	36%
Gen X	26%	27%	29%
Boomers	34%	26%	28%

Source: Theos/ Faraday/ YouGov 2022: Overall Population [n= 5153], Nones [n =2705], Campaigning Nones [n = 601]

Campaigning Nones follow a similar generational pattern as Nones overall, with the majority being Millennials. However, we have noticed Campaigning Nones have proportionately slightly more individuals in Gen X and Boomers than Nones overall, indicating that they are *marginally* older than Spiritual Nones.

Just as Spiritual Nones are heavily women, Campaigning Nones are disproportionately male (68% men vs 32% women). Most individuals in this group possess a high level of science knowledge, with 57% of individuals obtaining a high science knowledge score compared with 44% of Nones overall. Moreover, Campaigning Nones are more confident in their science knowledge than Nones overall, with 50% of them (and only 32% of Nones overall) being highly confident in their science knowledge.

Campaigning Nones, unlike Nones overall and Spiritual Nones have very low levels of belief in anything spiritual/supernatural, with 80% of this cluster stating they do not believe in anything spiritual or supernatural.

This group does fit into the stereotypical ideas of Nones. They are a group of individuals who state their motives and beliefs about the world are ruled by "science, logic, and evidence and rationality." They often hold a scientistic and naturalistic view of the world.

Campaigning Nones are disproportionately male.

Their attitude to knowledge

Campaigning Nones' attitude towards the world — and in turn religion — is motivated by their strong faith in the authority of science. This is witnessed in the fact that 78% believe that science is the only way of getting reliable knowledge about the world, with a further 45% agreeing that science will be able to explain everything one day (vs 36% of Nones overall and 27% of Spiritual Nones).

In a similar way, Campaigning Nones are a group of individuals who believe that science can dictate and inform how you live your life, with 25% believing that "Science can tell you how to live your life" (vs 16% of Spiritual Nones).

Moreover, this group is not only certain of their belief in science and its capabilities to explain the natural world, but also thinks of science as less fallible than other forms of knowledge (Figure 12).

Figure 12: "Science is less affected by bias and error than other human activities": by Nones Cluster

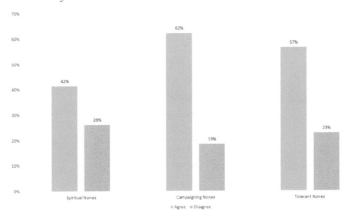

Source: Theos/ Faraday/ YouGov 2022: Q1_11 (Spiritual Nones [n= 601], Campaigning Nones [n= 618], Tolerant Nones [n= 664])

Campaigning Nones are most consistently 'pro–science'; although this does not mean that other clusters are against science. Rather, it suggests that Campaigning Nones have a deep conviction and belief in the authority of science as a form of knowledge upon which to base one's understanding of the world.

Their belief about God

Most Campaigning Nones (79%) do not believe in God (vs 51% of Nones overall and 11% of Spiritual Nones), although 18% qualify as agnostic (See Figure 13).

Figure 13: Campaigning Nones' beliefs about God

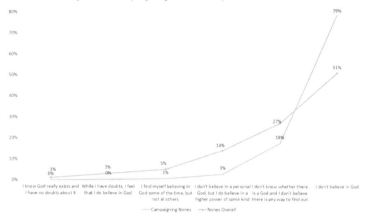

Source: Theos/ Faraday/ YouGov 2022: Q16 (Nones [n=2705], Campaigning Nones [n= 618])

Their belief about religion and the Bible

Campaigning Nones have an extremely hostile stance towards religion.

89% of Campaigning Nones agree, "Religion has no place in the modern world".

Unlike the Spiritual Nones group, 80% of whom believe in some form of the spiritual/ supernatural, 80% of Campaigning Nones do not believe in any form of spirituality or the supernatural. However, that also means that, even among this most sceptical of groups, there are 20% that appear to believe in some form of the supernatural/ spiritual.

This attitude is matched (even exceeded) by that towards religion. 89% of Campaigning Nones agree, "Religion has no place in the modern world" (see Figure 14).

Figure 14: Religion has no place in the modern world: by Nones Cluster

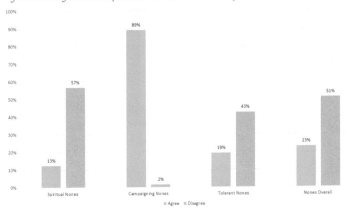

Source: Theos/ Faraday/ YouGov 2022: Q2c_3 (Spiritual Nones [n= 601], Campaigning Nones [n= 618], Tolerant Nones [n= 664], Nones Overall [n= 2705])

We can see that there is a drastic difference between Campaigning Nones and the other groups of Nones (and indeed Nones overall) about what they think of religion and its place in society. Campaigning Nones are the most hostile to religion, with them not only believing that religion has no

There is a drastic difference between Campaigning Nones and the other groups of Nones about what they think of religion and its place in society.

place in the modern world but also that it is a form of child abuse and a deadly virus (Figure 15).

Figure 15: Hostility to Religion: by Nones Cluster

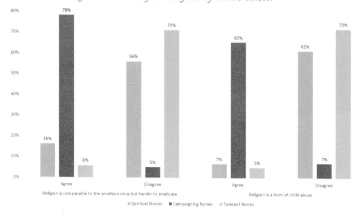

Source: Theos/ Faraday/ YouGov 2022: Q2c_6 & Q2c_7 (Spiritual Nones [n= 601], Campaigning Nones [n= 618], Tolerant Nones [n = 664])

In this sense then, Campaigning Nones are not only against religion in the modern world, but they are against religion in all forms. Religion is, for individuals in this group, a form of evil that does considerable damage to children who are exposed to it and is a virus that needs to be eradicated from society.

Predictably, regarding the Bible, 78% of Campaigning Nones agree "Science disproves the Bible" compared to only 33% of Spiritual Nones and 55% of Tolerant Nones. Similarly, the individuals within this group also hold a highly negative view of Holy Texts, with most viewing the Bible as "an irrelevant collection of ancient myths" (Figure 16). It is also worth noting that Campaigning Nones are the more likely to voice their opinions regarding the Bible compared to Nones overall (and the other two clusters).

Figure 16: Campaigning Nones' beliefs about the Bible

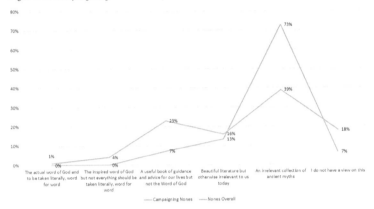

Source: Theos/ Faraday/ YouGov 2022: Q17 (Campaigning Nones [n= 618], Nones overall [n= 2705])

Summary

Campaigning Nones are the Nones that many individuals typically picture when someone describes themselves as atheist. They are those who see religion as a source of evil in the world, and believe they have a duty to tell people of its dangers and "campaign" for atheism. It is this kind of None that has captured headlines in the last 15 years or so and our research confirms that this is not simply a caricature but a position and range of views that is genuinely held by some – although, importantly, not by all - non-religious people.

'TOLERANT NONES'

Cluster 3. Tolerant Nones

The final group of Nones that we were able to identify are those who we have called *Tolerant Nones*.

Tolerant Nones:

— have the highest levels of education out of all the clusters;
— are spiritually closed;
— believe that science cannot tell you how to live your life;
— are generally atheistic in their belief about God, although around a quarter are agnostic;
— are more tolerant and accepting of religion than Campaigning Nones;
— believe religion has some helpful things to say about ethics.

Table 3: Generational Trends of Overall Population, Nones Overall and Tolerant Nones

	Overall Population	Nones Overall	Tolerant Nones
Gen Z	9%	10%	11%
Millennial	32%	37%	40%
Gen X	26%	27%	24%
Boomers	34%	26%	25%

Source: Theos/ Faraday/ YouGov 2022: Overall Population [n =5153], Nones [n =2705], 'Tolerant Nones' [n = 601]

Tolerant Nones follow a similar generational pattern as Nones overall with the majority being Millennials. We have found that Tolerant Nones have the highest proportion of Millennials of the three clusters and a very slightly higher proportion of Gen Z, suggesting that they are the youngest of the clusters.

Unlike the Spiritual Nones and Campaigning Nones, Tolerant Nones are spread relatively evenly across gender (53% male and 47% female). Tolerant Nones are spiritually closed; with 82% stating they do not believe in anything spiritual (vs. 58% of Nones overall, 20% of Spiritual Nones and 80% of

Campaigning Nones). In this way, this group of individuals view spirituality in a similar manner to Campaigning Nones but approach spirituality and religion in quite different ways.

Their education

Tolerant Nones are the most educated out of the clusters, with 52% finishing their formal education after the age of 20 (compared to 41% of Nones overall, 42% of Campaigning Nones and 39% of Spiritual Nones).

Individuals in this cluster possess the highest-level science knowledge compared to the other two clusters, with 61% obtaining a high science knowledge score compared to 57% of Campaigning Nones, 31% of Spiritual Nones and 44% of Nones overall. However, despite them possessing the highest levels of science knowledge they are not as confident in their knowledge of science as Campaigning Nones.[5] Tolerant Nones also possess the highest levels of religion knowledge score with 33% obtaining a high religion knowledge score compared to 25% of Nones overall, 28% of Campaigning Nones and 24% of Spiritual Nones. We assessed if this was due to individuals in this group having received a higher level of formal education in science and religion. However, we found no significant differences.

Their attitude to knowledge

Tolerant Nones are a group that are difficult to pin down when it comes to their epistemology. 71% of them agree that "Science is the only reliable way of getting knowledge about the world" – less than the 78% of Campaigning Nones who agree, but more than the 48% of Spiritual Nones. This

Tolerant Nones are the most educated.

suggests that individuals within this group may subscribe to a scientific and naturalistic epistemology of the world, but that it isn't quite as much a part of their identity or outlook on life as it is with Campaigning Nones.

If we pair the previous finding with the fact that 63% of Tolerant Nones agree, "Science cannot tell you how to live your life" (vs 59% of Spiritual Nones, 45% of Campaigning Nones and 53% of Nones overall), it seems to suggest that, despite their strong level of trust in science's ability to discern the world, this group do draw the line at morality, having confidence in science but also recognising its limits (Figure 17).

Figure 17: Beliefs about science: by Nones Cluster

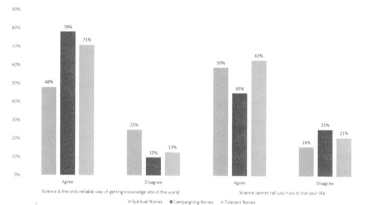

Source: Theos/ Faraday/ YouGov 2022: Q1_2, & Q1_13, (Spiritual Nones [n= 601], Campaigning Nones [n= 618], Tolerant Nones [n= 664])

This point is supported by the fact that 54% of Tolerant Nones believe that there are some things science will never be able to explain, and 50% state that science is only able to explain part of reality. When we compared these results with

Spiritual and Campaigning Nones, it appears that Tolerant Nones inhabit a space between these two clusters, with 64% of Spiritual Nones and 42% of Campaigning Nones agreeing that science is only able to explain part of reality and 77% of Spiritual Nones and 43% of Campaigning Nones believing that there are some things science will never be able to explain.

It certainly seems then that Tolerant Nones appear to sit in the middle of Spiritual and Campaigning Nones when it comes to epistemology. Tolerant Nones see the value and importance of science and indeed view it is as the most and/ or only reliable way of getting knowledge about the world. However, this does not mean that individuals in this group are committed to science in the way that Campaigning Nones are. They recognise and place importance and significance on the scientific approach but do not believe that this means science can tell an individual how to live their life.

Tolerant Nones appear to sit in the middle of Spiritual and Campaigning Nones when it comes to epistemology.

Their belief about God

Like Campaigning Nones, the vast majority of Tolerant Nones do not believe in God (Figure 18). However, they tend to hold slightly more varied opinions regarding God than Campaigning Nones, with the same proportion of Tolerant and Spiritual Nones stating, "I don't know whether there is a God, and I don't believe there is any way to find out" (29%). In this respect, we can understand Tolerant Nones as individuals who are a bit less atheistic than Campaigning Nones, but less open to spirituality and agnosticism than Spiritual Nones.

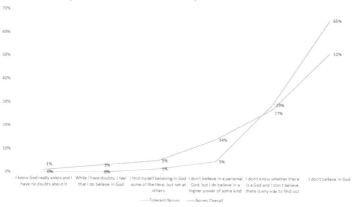

Figure 18: Tolerant Nones' beliefs about God

Source: Theos/ Faraday/ YouGov 2022: Q16 (Tolerant Nones [n = 664], Nones Overall [n =2705])

Their belief about religion

43% of Tolerant Nones disagree with the statement "Religion has no place in the modern world" compared with 57% of Spiritual Nones – and only 2% of Campaigning Nones! Furthermore, we found that Tolerant Nones disagree most strongly – even more so that Spiritual Nones – with the statements: "Religion is a form of child abuse" and "Religion is comparable to the smallpox virus but harder to eradicate" (Figure 19).

Figure 19: Hostile Views of Religion: by Nones Cluster

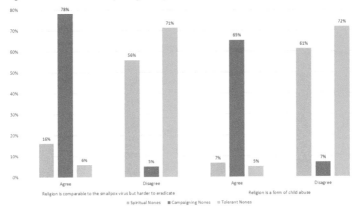

Source: Theos/ Faraday/ YouGov 2022: Q2c_6 and Q2c_7, (Spiritual Nones [n= 601], Campaigning Nones [n= 618], Tolerant Nones [n= 664])

In this way we can see that although Tolerant Nones are just as atheistic as Campaigning Nones, they are nothing like as negative towards religion. They are still atheistic Nones, but they are not as crusading or committed to ridding the world

of religion. This group of Nones are more tolerant towards religion, even recognising its potential for positive moral and social contribution, and embody the idea of 'live and let live'.

This serves to demonstrate that individuals who do not believe in God do not always hold hostile views towards religion.

Tolerant Nones show us that individuals who do not believe in God do not always hold hostile views towards religion.

Tolerant Nones not only hold a more positive view of religion and its place in society, but most of those within this group (38%) believe that "All religions have some element of truth in them" (14% of Campaigning Nones and 59% of Spiritual Nones). The fact individuals see some elements of truth within religion may influence how they view religious input into ethics, with 65% of Tolerant Nones disagreeing with the statement that "Religion has nothing helpful to say about ethics", compared with 55% of Spiritual Nones and 16% of Campaigning Nones. In this way, it is more accurate to say that individuals within this group do not believe in God/spirituality or the supernatural, but they think parts of religion are not only truthful, but beneficial to society when it comes ethics and morality.

Interestingly, this group of individuals is divided on what they think of the Bible with 32% viewing the Bible as "A useful book of guidance and advice for our lives but not the Word of God" and 32% viewing it as "An irrelevant collection of ancient myths" (Figure 20).

Figure 20: Tolerant Nones views on the Bible

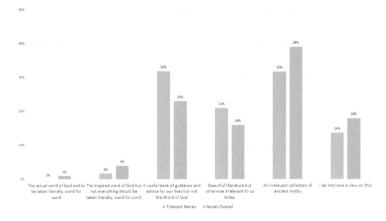

Source: Theos/ Faraday/ YouGov 2022: Q17, (Tolerant Nones [n = 664], Nones Overall [n= 2705])

Summary

Tolerant Nones highlight the diversity of opinions in Nones who are clearly atheists. The people in this this cluster are neither spiritual nor religious, and they do not believe in God but that does not stop them in seeing value and worth in religion. Finally, they are a group of individuals who embody the ideology of 'live and let live', though they do not believe in God or spirituality they are unlike campaigning atheists, as they are not trying to belittle, argue against or rid the world of religion. Instead, they are accepting of religion and see it as having a justified place in society.

1   A hierarchical cluster solution demonstrated three distinct clusters of Nones, and we further examined these clusters through a K-means cluster analysis. We found that K-means cluster performed better than hierarchical cluster analysis, providing a more in-depth and robust insight into the three clusters. K-Means clustering is a method of statistical analysis that groups similar data points into a cluster. It does this by finding the similarity between items, in this case, responses to certain questions and groups them together into various clusters.

2   The statements selected were to what extent you agree/ disagree: "All religions have some element of truth in them", "Religion has nothing helpful to say about ethics," "Religion is comparable to the smallpox virus but harder to eradicate", "Religion has no place in the modern world," "Humans are at heart spiritual beings" and "Religion is a form of child abuse". We also selected statements regarding the extent to which individuals believe in life after death, heaven, hell, religious miracles, reincarnation, nirvana, angels, ghosts, the power of prayer, the healing power of crystals and the supernatural power of ancestors. We selected questions regarding religious practices asking participants: "How often do you pray?" (Several times a day, once a day, several times a week, every week, occasional, never). We also included "How often do you attend religious services?" (Once a week or more, less often but at least once in two weeks, less often but at least once a month, less than once a month, never or practically never). "Which best described your beliefs about God? ("I know God really exists and I have no doubts about it", "While I have doubts, I feel that I do believe in God", "I find myself believing in God some of the time, but not at others", "I don't believe in a personal God, but I do believe in a higher power of some kind", "I don't know whether there is a God, and I don't believe there is any way to find out", "I don't believe in God".) Finally, we included a statement regarding the Bible in which participants were asked: "Which statement comes closest to your feelings about the Bible? The Bible is…? ("The actual word of God and to be taken literally, word for word", "The inspired word of God but not everything should be taken literally, word for word", "Is a useful book of guidance and advice for our lives but no the Word of God", "Is beautiful literature but otherwise irrelevant to us today", "Is an irrelevant collection of ancient myths" and "I do not have a view on this".)

3   The clusters have been rounded up to a single percentage without decimals leading to a calculated total of 101%, this is because the total number of Campaigning Nones is 33.5% and Tolerant Nones is 34.5% (rounded up as 34% and 35% respectively).

4   To assess levels of belief we analysed if individuals believed in any of the following: life after death, heaven, hell, religious miracles, reincarnation, nirvana, angels, ghosts, the power of prayer, the healing power of crystals and supernatural power of ancestors.

5 Only 41% of individuals in this group are highly confident in their science knowledge (36% moderately confident and 23% have low confidence) compared to 50% of antagonistic atheists who are highly confident in their science knowledge (29% moderately confident and 21% low confidence).

Conclusion

Overall, this research has highlighted not only an interesting insight into who the Nones are in the UK today but also provides some insight into different ways to be a None.

The research provides a nuanced approach to understanding the non-religious and demonstrates that the stereotypical view that Nones are vehemently against religion, spirituality and God is a far cry from the truth. Rather, we have found a diversity of opinions in the three clusters presented in this report.

> 66
>
> ---
>
> **The stereotypical view that Nones are vehemently against religion, spirituality and God is a far cry from the truth.**

The first of the clusters – Spiritual Nones – have demonstrated that there are individuals in the UK who are indeed non-religious, but this does not mean they are non-spiritual or non-supernatural. Instead, we find a group of people with varied levels of belief in deities, fate, karma, or a higher power. This may be because individuals in this group think that at their core, humans are spiritual beings.

Spiritual Nones are a group of individuals who identify themselves as non-religious, but this does not mean they do not believe in God. Rather, it highlights that they have an agonistic approach to religion (which may also contribute to why they are more agreeable to religion's place in society).

Spiritual Nones are also what we have deemed epistemological pluralists. They are a group of individuals who value different forms of knowledge as authoritative in how one comes to understand the world and their place in it. It is because of this openness to epistemological pluralism that Spiritual Nones may be more accepting of religion in modern society and believe elements of it are truthful. As such, Spiritual Nones are not individuals who are religious, but they are a cluster of individuals who believe there are a variety of meaningful, authoritative, and fulfilling ways to understand the world, and that religion may be one of them. This is not to say that religion, or any specific part of religion(s) plays a large part in their own epistemology, but it is to say that they are comfortable with the fact that meaning, and knowledge can come from a variety of sources.

The second cluster we identified was that of Campaigning Nones. Campaigning Nones are not only extremely atheistic but also extremely hostile to religion, its content and place within society, with many of them viewing religion as a form of child abuse.

A significant part of Campaigning Nones' antagonism to religion is rooted in their scientific epistemology. Individuals within this group have a highly scientistic epistemology, meaning that science is viewed as the only means of attainting legitimate knowledge about the world. This means that individuals within this group believe that science is supreme and sufficient to describe the world, and if science is not able to explain something, it is not worth explaining. It is a deep core belief that science will and can explain everything.

Campaigning Nones inhabit this epistemology and as such are deeply concerned with the physical and natural world. As there is no material evidence to prove the existence of the supernatural, many in this group are convinced that religion is nothing more than a 'cop-out'. Religion is not an entity that is able to be tried, tested, and verified. In this sense, it is clear that because of Campaigning Nones' commitment to scientism, it is highly unlikely that they will view religion as anything of substance.

The final cluster we identified was the Tolerant Nones. The Tolerant Nones are individuals who are atheists and not at all spiritual, but they are accepting of religion, with many of them seeing its value in society. They are a group of individuals who inhabit a pluralistic epistemology like that of the Spiritual Nones, but also view science as a significant and authoritative voice. They are a group of individuals who can see value in religion and its place within society.

Understanding people who tick the 'not religious' box as simply atheists, or alternatively that they are all "Spiritual but not religious" does a disservice to them.

It is perhaps helpful to understand these clusters are on a spectrum, where Tolerant Nones sit between Spiritual and Campaigning Nones.

Figure 21: Spectrum of Nones

'SPIRITUAL NONES'   'TOLERANT NONES'   'CAMPAIGNING NONES'

If we are to begin to understand what it means to be non-religious in Britain today, we need to understand the subtle (and sometimes not so subtle) differences within these groups. Understanding people who tick the 'not religious' box as simply atheists, or alternatively that they are all "Spiritual but not religious" does a disservice to them. As we begin to understand the Nones more fully, we not only discover a variety of thoughts and opinions, but different flavours of Nones. Paying attention to these different flavours may enable us as a society to have better conversations about religion and its place in the modern world.

Theos – enriching conversations

Theos exists to enrich the conversation about the role of faith in society.

Religion and faith have become key public issues in this century, nationally and globally. As our society grows more religiously diverse, we must grapple with religion as a significant force in public life. All too often, though, opinions in this area are reactionary or ill informed.

We exist to change this

We want to help people move beyond common misconceptions about faith and religion, behind the headlines and beneath the surface. Our rigorous approach gives us the ability to express informed views with confidence and clarity.

As the UK's leading religion and society think tank, we reach millions of people with our ideas. Through our reports, events and media commentary, we influence today's influencers and decision makers. According to *The Economist*, we're "an organisation that demands attention". We believe Christianity can contribute to the common good and that faith, given space in the public square, will help the UK to flourish.

Will you partner with us?

Theos receives no government, corporate or denominational funding. We rely on donations from individuals and organisations to continue our vital work. Please consider signing up as a Theos Friend or Associate or making a one off donation today.

Theos Friends and Students

— Stay up to date with our monthly newsletter

— Receive (free) printed copies of our reports

— Get free tickets to all our events

£75/ year
for Friends

£40/ year
for Students

Theos Associates

— Stay up to date with our monthly newsletter

— Receive (free) printed copies of our reports

— Get free tickets to all our events

— Get invites to private events with the Theos team and other Theos Associates

£375/ year

Sign up on our website:
www.theosthinktank.co.uk/about/support-us